T0145149

A Roadmap for Planning

an in person and virtual family reunion during a pandemic

Ronald W. Holmes, Ph.D.

AuthorHouse™
1663 Liberty Drive
Bloomington, IN 47403
www.authorhouse.com
Phone: 833-262-8899

Because of the dynamic nature of the Internet, any web addresses or links contained in this book may have changed since publication and may no longer be valid. The views expressed in this work are solely those of the author and do not necessarily reflect the views of the publisher, and the publisher hereby disclaims any responsibility for them.

Any people depicted in stock imagery provided by Getty Images are models, and such images are being used for illustrative purposes only.
Certain stock imagery © Getty Images.

This book is printed on acid-free paper.

ISBN: 978-1-6655-2021-8 (sc)
ISBN: 978-1-6655-2022-5 (e)

Library of Congress Control Number: 2021905580

Print information available on the last page.

Published by AuthorHouse 03/24/2021

authorHOUSE

TABLE OF CONTENTS

A Roadmap for Planning an in person and virtual family reunion during a pandemic

Winona J. Johnson, Illustrator

ACKNOWLEDGEMENT

For the past 55 years, my family has conducted the Holmes Family Reunion. Due to the coronavirus pandemic in 2020, we conducted our reunion virtually. Over the past four years, my family has asked that I write a book to document the success of our family reunion. While I had started contemplating and gathering information about family reunions, it was not until the pandemic that I saw a strong reason and strategic way to write this book.

As a Holmes family member, I am delighted to share some best practices and processes that any family can use to plan a family reunion to communicate, network, and unite with loved ones for support and comfort.

Roadmap
Family Reunion

INTRODUCTION

In one of the The O'Jays' famous songs titled *"Family Reunion,"* the group sings about the significance and importance of a family reunion. Some of the lyrics reveals that, "It's so nice to see all the folks you love together, sitting and talking about all the things that are going down. At least once a year, we should have a family reunion."

This book provides a roadmap for planning an in person and virtual family reunion. It provides examples from my Holmes family from Leslie, Georgia; as well as the Batson family from Marianna, Florida; the Cardamone family from Raleigh, North Carolina; the Coleman family from Mound Bayou, Mississippi; the Crawford family from Barnswell, South Carolina; and the Hagans family from Geneva, Alabama.

WHAT IS A FAMILY REUNION?

A family reunion is an occasion when a great number of members of an immediate and extended family come together to fellowship with each other. This event is typically conducted yearly or every two years during the same time of the year. The event often includes a meal, activities, and discussions on a variety of topics. Attendees might include members from the older generation such as grandparents, parents, siblings, and first cousins. Attendees could include members from the younger generation such as the second, third, and fourth cousins providing them an opportunity to learn more about their family and history. Attendees could also include friends of the family supporting those who may not have a regular family reunion.

On July 4, 1965, The Holmes family conducted its first family reunion at the home of Victoria Holmes in Leslie, Georgia. This landmark gathering was under a big oak tree. On this day, our grandmother Victoria gave the charge to her children to keep the families meeting every year around the Fourth of July with emphasis on prayer, singing, fellowship, worship, and an abundance of love. To this date, the legacy lives on through the descendants of Lynwood and Victoria Holmes.

In 1989, the Batson reunion started in Marianna, Florida. The Batson's decision was made because elder family members were passing, and members of the family wanted to capture their history from the elders and ancestors.

The Cardamone reunion started in 1996 at a lake house in Raleigh, North Carolina. The tradition started with a great aunt baking apple pies. Family members would bring large bags of apples to the aunt to bake the pies.

The Coleman family who hail from Mound Bayou, Mississippi conducted its first family reunion in Detroit, Michigan in 2001. The tradition started with a nephew communicating with his aunt that he did not know his family and wanted to have a family reunion. This aunt being receptive to his concern subsequently planned the Coleman's first family reunion.

The Crawford's reunion started in Barnswell, South Carolina in 1940 through the legacy of a grandfather in his young age. The reunion included former slaves and white family members.

The planning for the first Hagans' family reunion occurred after the funeral of Alford Hagans while in Geneva, Alabama in 1955. Fred Hagans, Alford's son, suggested that the family should not get together for only funerals and weddings; they should get together on a more regular basis. The decision was made that the reunions should be held every two years and alternate between a southern and northern location so no family would experience exorbitant travel costs. Hosting of the reunions would rotate among the children of Alford and Roxie Hagans. The reunion would be held on the weekend closest to July 10-12, the anniversary of the birth and death of their mother, Roxie Hagans. The first reunion was hosted by Marie Hagans Tanner in Panama City, Florida.

BENEFITS OF A FAMILY REUNION

While there are many benefits of a family reunion, the Holmes Family Reunion allows us to visit with family and friends in various parts of the United States. It allows us to learn from family, friends and elders particularly through chats, meetings, seminars, programs, and church services. It allows us to offer scholarships to family members attending college. It also allows us to review information from the previous reunions so we can effectively organize for future reunions and maintain our family tradition. Over the past 55 years, it has been a blessing to come together, fellowship, and celebrate with our family at a reunion. The experience has broadened our relationships with family members given us a better awareness of our diverse relatives who work in great professions and live across the world.

Cont- BENEFITS OF A FAMILY REUNION

According to the Batson, the benefits of the reunion is getting to know who they are, where they came from, and what they are doing today. Through the reunion, the achievements of family members (business, military, professional, etc.) are recognized to show the generations the successes and good genes of family members. They see the reunion as an opportunity to support each other and role model the success for the younger generation.

A great family reunion benefit for the Cardamone family is meeting and having fun with family members at its lake house in Raliegh, North Carolina. The time spent and having fun together with family members is also a benefit of the Coleman family. The opportunity to get away from home, learn how family members are doing, come together and see family members you don't know, and meet people who your parents have talked about over the years are benefits for the Crawford family. Also, the chance to get to know family members and learn about the great things they have accomplished and done in life (such as an aunt traveling to Haiti) are benefits for the Hagans family.

DOCUMENTING FAMILY HISTORY

One of the best ways for documenting your family history is with Ancestry.com. This online resource can help you learn about your family history through family trees, historical records, and DNA testing.

Documenting your family history can help you better understand yourself, feel closer to your family members, and better understand your family dynamics. Documenting your family history can also enable you to discover ancestors who you did not know, show you how they looked during a particular era, learn about their experiences in life, and preserve information about the ancestors for future generations.

The Holmes family history is celebrated and remembered through the legacy of Lynwood Holmes and Victoria Smith Holmes. They were blessed with 10 beautiful children comprising of six boys (Willie, Crawford, R.B., Walter, Lynwood, and Benjamin) and four girls (Lucille, Eleanor, Izora, and Ginnie). Before his untimely death in 1943, Lynwood was a great husband, a very good gospel singer, an excellent provider for his family, and a servant of the Lord who trained his children to believe in Jesus, pray, seek, and serve the Lord. Before her death in 1966, Victoria was a visionary, devoted wife, wonderful mother, shrewd business woman, and God fearing Christian.

Before the Internet, family members gathered information from the Courthouse to record the Holmes family tree (See Appendix A). In documenting our family history, a family profile was created and placed in the 50th Holmes Family Reunion Banquet Program. This historical document featured the profile of the descendants of Crawford Holmes and Queen Tondee; and Henrietta Floyd and Green Smith the parents of Lynwood Holmes and Victoria Smith Holmes respectively. Also, the document featured a family profile of the descendants of Lynwood Holmes and Victoria Smith Holmes including the second, third, fourth, and fifth generations. Family members collectively provided the names of each family member from the respective branches of the Holmes family along with special attributes about the parents. Since 1983, the Holmes family started documenting the family tree on its family reunion t-shirts. Over the years, the family has relied on members to recite the family history at its family reunion events.

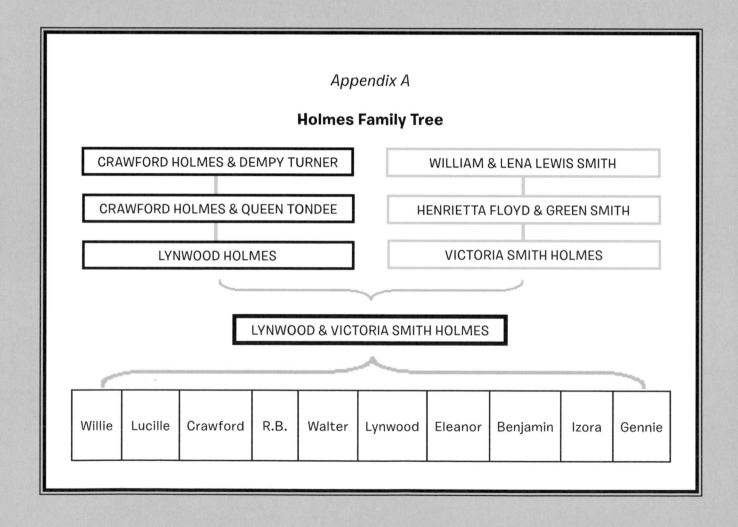

Appendix A

Holmes Family Tree

CRAWFORD HOLMES & DEMPY TURNER	WILLIAM & LENA LEWIS SMITH
CRAWFORD HOLMES & QUEEN TONDEE	HENRIETTA FLOYD & GREEN SMITH
LYNWOOD HOLMES	VICTORIA SMITH HOLMES

LYNWOOD & VICTORIA SMITH HOLMES

Willie	Lucille	Crawford	R.B.	Walter	Lynwood	Eleanor	Benjamin	Izora	Gennie

SELECTING THE RIGHT COORDINATOR

One of the first steps in planning a family reunion is selecting a coordinator. It is a good idea to select a coordinator who has good planning skills and the ability to work well with others in fulfilling all the responsibilities for conducting a reunion. The Holmes family has been fortunate to have such characteristics of a coordinator during the duration of its family reunions. The coordinator is responsible for developing a committee of people usually in the reunion city to meet, plan, and determine the logistics and activities for the reunion. Some of the logistics could include the necessary facilities, equipment, and supplies for coordinating the reunion. Some of the activities might include the necessary events for children, teenagers, adults, and senior citizens to foster a positive reunion gathering. The coordinator might also be responsible for establishing a database of family members, updating the database yearly, and using the database to contact family members about the reunion in person, via telephone, email, or social media outlets such as Facebook.

While the Holmes Family Reunion is held for approximately four to five days, the coordinator for the reunion and the committee members are always committed and prepared to effectively host the reunion in its city location. Some specific responsibilities include establishing and negotiating a cost and fee for the reunion activities (hotel, banquet, picnic, reception, t-shirts as cited in Appendix B); working closely with management at the hotel; assisting family with travel arrangements to the hotel; making sure rooms are available and accessible to family; troubleshooting any complaints about the hotel and its amenities; determining food requirements for activities; establishing a meet and greet event; registering family for the reunion; and providing family a calendar of events for the reunion.

The Batson family welcomes volunteers to host the reunion and support the volunteers without having to use a voting process. The host committee decides two years in advance where the next two reunions will be held. For budgetary reasons, seed money is collected from the family for the host committee. The committee creates an account for the year of the reunion and sets a budget for the events. The committee determines the cost of the activities, the deposits for the hotel, t-shirts, and mailings. The committee also determines the cost per person to attend the reunion and advises the family of the cost.

The Cardamone family does not charge or collect money for the family reunion. Family members bring food for the reunion cookout at the lake house in the country outside of Raleigh, North Carolina. Some members stay at the lake house while others stay at the hotel in Raleigh.

At the end of a family reunion, the Coleman family meets and determines where the next reunion will be held. When there are two or more volunteers seeking to host the reunion, the family votes and decides on the reunion location. The host committee plans the reunion, and informs family of the cost to attend the reunion. If there is a remaining balance, the money is provided to the next host committee as seed money.

At the end of each family reunion, the Crawford family determines where the next reunion will be held through volunteers who have the interest to host the reunion. Money is collected at the family reunion banquet to assist the planning for the next reunion programs and activities. Once the host is established, host committee sends information to family members providing them choices of cities and places to have the reunion, as well as activities. The host committee collects funds and handles the bills in coordinating the reunion. The committee sends reunion packets to family members with a breakdown of reunion fees. As a benefit, the host committee receives the complimentary room at the reunion hotel.

The Hagans' reunion is coordinated through a chairperson and planning committee. The committee agrees to where the reunion will be held along with the activities. The committee decides the fees based on the activities and t-shirt cost. The children's fees are half-price, and the hotel rate is reduced if booked as a family conference. Also, the host committee establishes an account when getting started. The money left over from the previous family reunion is used as seed money for the next committee to plan the reunion.

Appendix B

Sample Responsibilities of Coordinator
for the Holmes Family Reunion

Hotel

Gain a favorable hotel conference rate based on a projected attendance of people

Ensure the contract is in writing detailing rates for: sleeping rooms, hospitality suite for duration of reunion, meet and greet reception, banquet, and parking

Ensure that banquet costs cover differences in price for children and adults

Reunion Fee

Establish a family reunion fee for adults and children to plan for the family reunion banquet, reception, t-shirts, picnic, and other activities such as entertainment and transportation; avoid reunion fees for children under six years of age

Picnic

Secure a location to conduct the picnic and consider how family members will get to the location

Determine if the picnic will be catered or prepared by family members

Develop an accurate number of picnic attendees as the number of attendees tends to be higher for the picnic

T-shirts

Include in the reunion communication a questionnaire regarding the t-shirt ordering process: number of t-shirts needed, sizes, and cost

Identify a vendor to produce the family reunion t-shirts

Design the t-shirt that fits the theme and locale of the reunion

Ensure that the names of the key family members are put on the back of the t-shirt

Order extra t-shirts and develop a process for distribution

SELECTING THE GEOGRAPHICAL LOCATIONS

Having a family reunion has been a wonderful and joyful vacation experience for the Holmes family. Our reunion is always held during the Fourth of July. Since its 1965 inaugural reunion at the home of Victoria Holmes in Leslie, Georgia, the experience has afforded an opportunity for us to learn from each other and promote our legacy through different reunion activities. During the early years, the Holmes Family Reunion remained in the South and alternated between Georgia and Florida. In the early 70's, the reunion traveled north to Gary, Indiana and Chicago, Illinois. As the families grew, more states and cities were added to the reunion rotation where family members lived. Since the inception, the reunion has traveled across the nation. The cities in Georgia (South) were Leslie, Smithville, Albany, Americus, Lake Blackshear, and Atlanta. In the state of Florida (South), the cities were Jacksonville, Tallahassee, and Miami. In the North, the cities were Gary, Indiana, and Chicago, Illinois. In the West, the cities were Dallas, Texas, San Antonio, Texas, and Las Vegas, Nevada. In the East, the city was Rochester, New York. Approximately, every four or five years the reunion is held in the founding state location of Georgia. In 2020, the reunion was scheduled for Washington, D.C. Because of the coronavirus pandemic, we conducted the reunion through Zoom.

Cont- **SELECTING THE GEOGRAPHICAL LOCATIONS**

The Batson family reunion is held every two years. The Batson decides two years in advance to determine where the next two reunions will be held. While the Batson family travels to different cities and states to participate in the family reunion of the host committee, every sixth year the reunion is held in the founding location of Marianna, Florida.

The Cardamone family reunion is held every year. The reunion location is at a lake house in the country outside of Raleigh, North Carolina.

The Coleman family reunion is held every two years in different cities and states such as Atlanta, Georgia; Detroit, Michigan; Louisville, Kentucky; Mound Bayou, Mississippi; Pigeon Forge, Tennessee; Seattle, Washington; Houston, Texas; and Wisconsin Dells, Wisconsin. In 2019, the Coleman family cruised on the Carnival Liberty. This experience included a departure from Orlando, Florida to Nassau and Freeport Bahamas.

The Crawford family reunion is held every two years. The reunion locations have included Augusta, Georgia; Barnswell, South Carolina; Jacksonville, Florida; Los Angeles, California; New Orleans, Louisiana; and Washington, D.C.

The Hagans family reunion is held every two years. During the reunion, the Hagans decides the location for the next reunion from the chairperson and planning committee of where the reunion will be held. In the northern and southern parts of the country, some of the reunion locations included Chicago, Illinois; Youngstown, Ohio; Boston, Massachusetts; Gulf Port, Mississippi; Tampa, Florida; Jacksonville, Florida; and West Palm Beach, Florida.

SELECTING THE ACTIVITIES

Since its inaugural family reunion at the home of Victoria, the Holmes Family Reunion has grown significantly to meet the interest of the attendees who often reserve this time for their vacation. The coordinators are mindful of this as they plan the reunions. Some activities of the reunion included a hotel meet and greet on the first day, a church service for worshiping, a banquet for celebrating the family history, and a seminar for enrichment and learning (See Appendices C and D). Other activities usually include a scholarship drawing and awards for students attending college, a tour bus for going to an amusement park such as Disney World, and a recreational park for a family picnic. For family unity, pride, and togetherness, we wear a specially designed t-shirts at the picnic displaying the year of the reunion. Afterwards, we take a family group picture through a professional photographer enabling family members to order individual copies from the photographer.

Cont- **SELECTING THE ACTIVITIES**

For the Batson family, cooking, baking, and eating are the most important activities of the reunion when it is held at the original home site in Marianna, Florida. At the picnic, the family participates in tug-a-war, sack races, card games, dominoes, and fishing. The family also plays the Batson Buggy Board. The game is played with three family members on a team. The three team members strap their left and right feet to the board and together they move forward. If they are not in unison, all three of them will fall. The first team to the finish line wins a prize. Other activities include family tours of the host city and visits to historic sites, museums, and parks. At the closing of the Batson reunion, there is a church service. This service includes a breakfast and memorial service led by a local or family pastor. In gathering its family history, the Batson family creates a yearly family journal that includes a wide range of family information from the past two years. The journal was established to show records of family happenings such as deaths, births, marriages, anniversaries, military services, corporate awards, and achievements. The journal also includes family recipes to highlight some of the good cooks in the family. At the end of the journal, is a family directory. Each family gets a copy of the journal in order to keep in touch with family members throughout the year.

The Cardamone enjoys its family reunion at a lake house in the country outside of Raleigh, North Carolina through baking apple pies and cooking foods such as hamburgers, hot dogs, and chicken. The family also has fun through fishing, swimming, water skiing, and watching the fire works on the lake from family members' boats. Having an activity to determine who baked the best tasting apple pie is the most successful activity of the Cardamone's reunion.

While the Coleman family participates in some of the traditional reunion activities, it tailors the activities to the location and usually involves some competitive fun. For the reunion in Louisville, Kentucky, the Coleman family had a derby hat competition. When staying in cabins at the Pigeon Forge Reunion, the family had a breakfast cooking competition judged by family members. During the Carnival Cruise reunion, the family had a door decoration competition and Karoke night.

The Hagans family engages in activities to get acquainted with each other. Some of these activities include games based on family history such as Bingo, Family Feud, and Jeopardy. As an incentive, the family gives prizes to the person who wins the game. The Hagans' key activities include a fish fry on Friday where everyone wears the t-shirt designed for that reunion, a picnic on Saturday, and a religious service and dinner on Sunday. After the dinner, the family conducts a business meeting to determine the location and dates of the next reunion and takes the family picture. The family makes a large puzzle of a family photo that the family puts together as a group. The family enjoys going on tours in each city where the reunion is held. The family's most successful activity was the river tour at the Chicago reunion. To document its legacy, the Hagans family has created five family history books with the first book being developed in 1986. The family has also created a family cookbook with recipes from grandparents and other family members. The family compiled a profile on each family member that includes the name, occupation, and age of the family members.

Appendix C

Sample of a Seminar
Held at the 49th Holmes Family Reunion
Rochester, New York 2014

SEMINAR TITLE: 10 STEP PLAN FOR WRITING A BOOK

INTRODUCTION

The following is a 10 Step Plan for publishing your own book. You can login to The Holmes Education Post (theholmeseducationpost.com) to read each of the chapters.

- ❖ DETERMINE AN AREA OF INTEREST

- ❖ RESEARCH AREA OF INTEREST WITH A FOCUS

- ❖ WRITE ABOUT AREA OF INTEREST WITH TIMELINE

- ❖ ESTABLISH A FILING SYSTEM OF MATERIALS FOR AREA OF INTEREST

- ❖ GROUP MATERIALS FOR AREA OF INTEREST

- ❖ DEVELOP INTRODUCTORY AND CLOSING FOR AREA OF INTEREST

- ❖ IDENTIFY EDITOR TO REVIEW ALL MATERIALS

- ❖ IDENTIFY PUBLISHING COMPANY FOR THE BOOK

- ❖ ESTABLISH A DESIGN FOR THE BOOK

- ❖ PUBLISH BOOK AND NOTIFY CONSTITUENTS

HINT:

Each chapter of this 10 Step Plan (free ebook) can be found in the Bookstore section of The Holmes Education Post.

Appendix D

Suggestion for a Family Reunion Seminar
A Family's Guide to Understanding the Coronavirus (COVID-19)

INTRODUCTION

This seminar teaches family members about the coronavirus (COVID-19) and ways to protect themselves and other people from the disease. The seminar covers three objectives:

1. What is COVID-19?

2. How does COVID-19 spread?

3. What actions can be taken to protect yourselves and others from getting the virus?

RESOURCES

A Free Demo of an Online Coronavirus Awareness Curriculum @ The Holmes Education Post (theholmeseducationpost.com)

A book entitled *Jacob's Dream! A Children's Guide to Understanding the Coronavirus (COVID-19)* by Ronald Holmes

COORDINATING A VIRTUAL FAMILY REUNION

In 2020, we experienced the height of the coronavirus pandemic. It was too dangerous from a health standpoint to assemble families as the Center for Disease Control and Prevention was advising everyone to shelter in place and not congregate. As a result, we wanted to continue honoring our tradition of seeing each other while remaining safe. Just as schools and businesses moved to using online virtual meetings, our reunion made the same transition. For the first time, we conducted a virtual reunion via Zoom. Our 55th reunion required the same planning but was conducted online. Family members received correspondence via email and Facebook about the process to login on Zoom. Subsequently, they participated in the reunion from their home city locations.

This experience was quite different, unique, and special since families were socially and physically separated from each other as result of the pandemic. Through the Zoom reunion, family members were overwhelmingly excited to see and talk to each other. To resemble our reunion tradition, we wore specially designed family reunion t-shirts displaying the year of the reunion. We also had a family reunion program as highlighted in Appendix E. The program comprised of guest speakers who provided enriching information to support the spiritual, social, and emotional needs of our family.

**Sample of The Holmes Family Reunion Program
Conducted through Zoom, 2020**

**Theme: Virtually Keeping the Legacy Alive!
Be on your guard; stand firm in the faith; be courageous; be strong
I Corinthians 16:13 NIV**

PRESIDING ....

OPENING REMARKS & INVOCATION..

WELCOME...

OCCASION ....

SCRIPTURE...

FAMILY SONG ....

FAMILY HISTORY..

FAMILY REFLECTIONS & NEWS ....

PANDEMIC SURVIVAL SKILLS...

SPECIAL MESSAGE ....

SPOKEN WORD...

SCHOLARSHIP PRESENTATION...

2020 FAMILY UPDATE...

CLOSING REMARKS..

ACKNOWLEDGEMENTS...

SPIRITURAL RAP SONG...

BENEDICTION...

Do everything in love. I Corinthians 16:14 NIV

Cont- COORDINATING A VIRTUAL FAMILY REUNION

In planning a Virtual Family Reunion through virtual meeting platforms such as Zoom, GoToMeeting, and Intrado, the following are some best practices you can follow:

❖ Establish coordinator and committee members for the family reunion

❖ Establish agenda for the Virtual Family Reunion program through coordinator and committee members

❖ Establish a virtual meeting account through platforms such as Zoom, GoToMeeting, and Intrado

❖ Become familiar with the technology for coordinating the family reunion through virtual meeting platforms in order to enhance visibility of speakers and eliminate unnecessary noise

❖ Notify family members of the family reunion program and process to login on the virtual meeting platform

❖ Encourage family members to login early (before the meeting starts) on the virtual meeting platform and become comfortable with using the mute button

❖ Limit the virtual meeting time to no more than 1.5 hours due to attention span

❖ Have coordinator or committee member to oversee family reunion program

❖ Evaluate the effectiveness of the family reunion program

❖ Determine coordinator and committee members for the next virtual family reunion

Sample of The Holmes Family Christmas Program
Conducted through Zoom, 2020

Scripture: Matthew 1:21 And she shall bring forth a Son, and thou shall call his name JESUS: For he shall save his people from their sins.

Master of Ceremony ....

Opening Prayer ....

What Christmas Means to Me ....

Musical Selection ....

The Importance of Academic Excellence ....

Musical Selection ....

Christmas Mask Reveal ....

Remarks and Closing Prayer ....

COORDINATING OTHER VIRTUAL FAMILY EVENTS

The virtual meeting platforms such as Zoom, GoToMeeting, and Intrado can be transferrable to other family events such as birthdays, Thanksgiving, and Christmas celebrations. My immediate family typically pulls names for Christmas gifts with the older family members and buys gifts for all of the younger members. We would meet in person on Christmas morning and exchange the gifts. Due to the pandemic, we held our Christmas celebration for the first time via Zoom. We broadened our gift exchange to our second generation of nieces and nephews who are all employed. We asked everyone to buy a gift of a mask that we thought would be useful to family members considering our COVID-19 environment. As a criteria, the coordinator of the event specifically asked everyone to think about the person's personality and buy a mask that he or she would enjoy wearing, mail the mask to the person, and state the reason he or she bought the mask for the person during the Zoom celebration. Also, the coordinator developed a program utilizing primarily the youth of the family from ages three to twenty eight. Appendix F provides a sample of the program for the Holmes' Christmas Celebration via Zoom.

COORDINATING A FAMILY REUNION CRUISE

Many families including the Holmes have expressed an interest in planning a family reunion cruise to expand their vacation experience. Compared to a reunion on land, the Coleman family found that the cruise was one of the easiest to plan and conduct.

In 2018, the Coleman family took a reunion cruise on Carnival to the Bahamas. The process started with the family working with the cruise line approximately 16 months ahead of the event and communicating with its family one year before the cruise. The following are the steps the family took for its maiden voyage:

- **Identified family members to work on the committee with a coordinator.** The Coleman family asked one person from each of the family branches to volunteer to help on the committee. The family especially wanted members who were familiar with cruising to participate to take advantage of their knowledge and contacts.

- **Conducted research on the cruise lines and costs.** The planning committee summarized this information on a spreadsheet and identified the items that were most important to the family. The committee's key information captured and decisions were:

  - Destination/Itinerary and length– What were the ports of call for the cruise line? Since this was a first time cruise for many, the committee decided to go with a shorter cruise of three days rather than the longer five –seven day cruise.

  - Departure City – The planning committee wanted to depart from a location that was easy for most family members to get to via car or flights. The committee chose to cruise out of Cape Canaveral because it allowed some family members to go to Disney in Orlando if they wanted a pre-cruise experience.

  - Cost - For many of the family members, this was going to be the first time they had ever taken a cruise. The planning committee did not want them to decide not to come due to price. The committee chose to go with the lowest cost cruise so that everyone could participate.

- **Registered cruise as a group cruise.** This meant that a planning committee coordinator worked with one key representative from the cruise line. The representative organized the cruise as a group which gave the Coleman family better rates and allowed the family to accumulate cruise points to cover various activities. The representative provided all of the information that needed to be shared with the family and all monies were provided directly to the cruise. Through the committee coordinator, the family was able to track who had paid and sent gentle reminders to family members along the way.

- **Payment -** All payments were sent directly to the cruise line. The Coleman family started the process one year before the cruise, and the cruise line gave the family a timeline for all monies to be paid. By the time the cruise occurred, all members had fully paid for their trip except for excursions and drinks.

Cont- COORDINATING A FAMILY REUNION CRUISE

- **Group dinners** – The Coleman family worked with the cruise line to eat all of its dinners together and in the same location each night. This allowed family members to go their separate ways during the day but have one time of the day to see all of the family. To accomplish this, the coordinator provided all of the names of the family members to the cruise line and a seating chart for the family.

- **Family Reception** – There are not many small rooms on the ship to have receptions so this had to be coordinated with the cruise representative from the beginning. Due to the number of people the Coleman family had in attendance, the family was able to use its cruise points to reserve rooms and to have hors d'oeuvres and drinks. This is also the time that the Coleman family conducted a short family program. The family had the room for one hour so it was important to remind family members that they had to begin and end on time.

- **T-shirts** – As with a typical family reunion, the Coleman's had a specially designed family reunion t-shirt. Due to this being a cruise reunion, there were some family members attending who had never been to a Coleman family reunion and thus, had never met family members before the cruise. The planning committee asked family members to wear their reunion t-shirt onto the cruise so that they were easily identifiable. The family also wore the shirts to dinner on the first night. This tactic worked well and the Coleman family received positive comments and lots of questions from other cruisers about how many were in its family.

- **Group Picture** – The Coleman family used its cruise points to have a professional cruise photograph taken which was immediately after the reception. The planning committee asked all of the family members to wear white. The family received two family photographs per cabin. The planning committee was responsible for distributing the (eight) 8 by 11 picture to all the family members on the cruise.

EVALUATING THE FAMILY REUNION

During and after the Holmes Family Reunion, the coordinator and committee members typically assess the effectiveness of the reunion by being receptive to positive and negative feedback from family members. This might include things family members were dissatisfied with at the reunion banquet such as food and service. This might also include things family members were satisfied with at the reunion such as hotel rooms or children playing on a playground at a family picnic. Subsequently, this information is shared with family members for better planning of the reunion in the foreseeable future.

As a recap, Appendix G provides key points for planning a family reunion. Also, Appendix H provides an evaluation form that families can use to assess the effectiveness of their family reunions.

Appendix G

Key Points for Planning a Family Reunion

❖ **Research Current Family History** – A family member who enjoys reading or engaging in research would be a good representative for his or her family.

❖ **Establish Current Purpose or Benefit for Family Reunion** –The purpose for having a family reunion can vary from one family to another. Sometimes the purpose can evolve from a strong elderly and spiritual family member who loves and values family togetherness and who can best set the tone for the family. Other times, it can evolve from a younger person who wants to learn about his or her family history.

❖ **Determine Location for Family Reunion** – The location of the reunion can vary depending on the climate, family history, purpose, and interest.

❖ **Establish Coordinator for Family Reunion** – A coordinator could be a family member who has good planning skills, works well with others, and makes sure that all family members receive the necessary details and correspondences about the family reunion. Some communications might include expenses to attend the reunion such as hotel, banquet, picnic, t-shirts, and entertainment. The coordinator will also establish and/or update the database of family members, and use the database to contact family members about the reunion in person, via telephone, email, or social media outlets such as Facebook.

❖ **Establish Committee Members to Work with the Coordinator** – Committee members could be any family members who are keenly interested in helping to plan the reunion in collaboration with the coordinator.

❖ **Plan Family Reunion Based on a Purpose Statement** – With a purpose statement, this is to help family members to be reminded of the reason for the family reunion so they can plan activities in accordance with the purpose statement.

❖ **Oversee Process for Family Reunion Once Planned** – The essential roles of the coordinator and committee members are to work collaboratively together to complete various tasks for the reunion and manage it at the highest level possible.

❖ **Celebrate the Family Reunion History and Tradition** – The pinnacle of the family reunion is to fellowship with each family member and celebrate the history and legacy of the family through a wide range of activities such as a picnic, banquet, worship service, and entertainment.

❖ **Evaluate the Effectiveness of the Family Reunion** – During and after the reunion, it is important that the coordinator and committee members assess the effectiveness of the reunion and share information (positive and negative) with the future coordinator and committee members.

❖ **Repeat Family Reunion Cycle and Make Changes When Necessary** – Considering the feedback gained from the coordinator and committee members, this provides the baseline information for improving the family reunions in the foreseeable future.

Sample Evaluation Form
For A Family Reunion

INSTRUCTIONS: Please rate items below related to your family reunion. The information will be used to improve future reunions.

Reunion Details	Ratings			
	Poor	**Fair**	**Good**	**Excellent**
1. Location of Reunion				
2. Hotel Accommodation				
3. Meals Provided				
4. Activities:				
a. Meet & Greet				
b. Picnic				
c. Banquet				
d. Tour				

5. What did you like most about the reunion?

_____

_____

_____

6. What did you like least about the reunion?

_____

_____

_____

7. What activities would you like for us to include at the next reunion?

_____

_____

_____

AUTHOR'S BACKGROUND

Ronald Holmes is the author of 23 books and publisher of "The Holmes Education Post," an education focused Internet newspaper. Holmes is a former teacher, school administrator, test developer, and district superintendent. He has written children books on the coronavirus, solar system, flowers, colors, careers, continents, animals, birds, bullying in school, and people and cultures from different countries. He has also written adults books on hazing, bipolar disorder, issues in education, and completing the dissertation.

IMAGES OF BOOKS BY RONALD W. HOLMES, Ph.D.

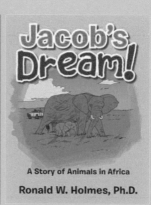
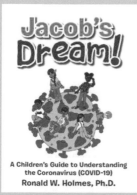

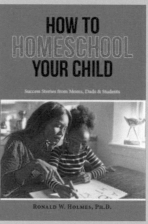

References

Holmes, B. (2017). Interviews of families' processes for conducting a family reunion. Jacksonville, FL.

Holmes, R. (2020). Jacob's Dream! A children guide to understanding the coronavirus (COVID-19). Bloomington, IN: Authorhouse.

Holmes, R. (2020). Jacob's Dream! A story on people and cultures from different countries. Bloomington, IN: Authorhouse.

Holmes, R. (2020). Jacob's Dream! A lesson on flowers and colors. Bloomington, IN: Authorhouse

Printed in the United States
by Baker & Taylor Publisher Services